GCSE Music
AQA Areas of Study

This book takes you through everything you need to know about the
Areas of Study for AQA's GCSE Music course.

Every topic is broken down into simple, manageable chunks,
so you know exactly what you need to learn.

What CGP is all about

Our sole aim here at CGP is to produce the highest quality
books — carefully written, immaculately presented and
dangerously close to being funny.

Then we work our socks off to get them out to you
— at the cheapest possible prices.

Contents

Section Five — AoS4: Timbre and Dynamics

Section Six — AoS5: Structure and Form

Section Seven — Bonus Track

Section Eight — Glossary and Index

Published by CGP

Main Authors:
John Deane
Elena Delaney
Faye Stringer

Further Contributors:
Polly Cotterill
Heather Gregson
Edmund Robinson
Caley Simpson

With thanks to Katherine Craig and Nikki Ball for the proofreading.

ISBN: 978 1 84762 371 3
Groovy website: www.cgpbooks.co.uk

Jolly bits of clipart from CorelDRAW®
Printed by Elanders Ltd, Newcastle upon Tyne

Based on the classic CGP style created by Richard Parsons.

What You Have to Do for GCSE Music

Music GCSE doesn't cover every single aspect of music — if it did it would take forever.
Instead you focus on five main 'Areas of Study' (AoS for short) and three strands of learning.

You Learn About Five Topics

AoS1 — RHYTHM AND METRE
(see Section 2)
For this one you look at things like simple and compound time, fancy rhythms and tempos.

AoS2 — HARMONY AND TONALITY (see Section 3)
In this AoS you learn about cadences, chords, keys and key changes. It also covers things like diatonic and chromatic harmony.

AoS3 — TEXTURE AND MELODY
(see Section 4)
This includes ways to make a melody more interesting, and covers the different textures that pieces can have.

AoS4 — TIMBRE AND DYNAMICS (see Section 5)
This one's about the timbres of different instruments and ways to play them. There are also some bits on dynamics.

AoS5 — STRUCTURE AND FORM (see Section 6)
This AoS covers the main structures used in music — things like binary and ternary form, and the structures of pop songs.

They Test You with an Exam...

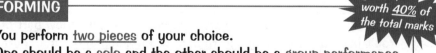

worth 20% of the total marks

At the end of Year 11 you do an exam called Listening to and Appraising Music. They test you across three Strands of Learning (topics that cover different types of music) — the Western Classical Tradition, Popular Music of the 20th and 21st Centuries and World Music. You'll have to answer questions on what you hear. You'll be tested on the five Areas of Study listed above.

The Areas of Study were discovered in 1483.

...and with Coursework

The coursework is work done during the course. Obviously. It's split into three chunks.

COMPOSING AND APPRAISING

worth 20% of the total marks

1) You compose one piece, linking it to two or more of the Areas of Study. It should also be linked to one of the strands listed above. The strand will be chosen by the exam board.
2) You then have to appraise your composition — that is, say why you chose to compose it and how successful it is. You'll have up to 2 hours of controlled time to fill in an appraisal booklet.

PERFORMING

worth 40% of the total marks

1) You perform two pieces of your choice.
2) One should be a solo and the other should be a group performance.

COMPOSING

worth 20% of the total marks

1) You have to compose another piece of music.
2) It also has to be linked to two or more Areas of Study, but it can be in any style you like.

Err, Miss... is it too late to change to physics?

Welcome to the wonderful world of GCSE Music. Breathe in the cool clear air. Listen to the birds. It's so beautiful, I could cry. Well actually, I couldn't, but it's OK compared to some subjects.

The Exam — Listening to and Appraising Music

Exams — my favourite. You have to sit a <u>one-hour exam</u> — it's called '<u>Listening to and Appraising Music</u>'.

The Listening Exam Tests All the Areas of Study

1) Unit 1 is the Listening Exam and it's worth <u>20%</u> of your total mark — that's a big chunk of marks.

2) As you might have guessed, it involves <u>listening</u>. The invigilator <u>plays music</u> from a CD. You listen to the music and answer <u>written questions</u> about it.

3) You'll have <u>two minutes</u> to look through the paper <u>before</u> the CD's played.

4) There are lots of <u>extracts</u> of music to listen to. Each one has its own set of <u>questions</u>. You'll hear a piece <u>at least twice</u>, and possibly up to five times (you'll be told how many times it'll be played). Do <u>all</u> the questions for it before moving on to the next one.

5) Some questions ask you to <u>compare</u> extracts — e.g. two different versions of the same piece. The question will tell you what <u>order</u> they'll be played in.

6) Concentrate on answering just a <u>few</u> of the questions each time the music's played — it's <u>less confusing</u>.

7) You <u>don't</u> get a lot of time on this paper, so <u>think fast</u> and <u>write fast</u>. There are <u>80 marks</u> available, but you only have <u>60 minutes</u> to do the exam — that's more than a mark a minute.

8) Each set of questions will focus mainly on <u>one Area of Study</u>, although they might ask you some bits about other ones too. The main <u>AoS</u> will be <u>shown</u> at the <u>beginning</u> of each set of questions.

Make sure you Read the Questions properly

1 Some questions are <u>multiple choice</u> — read all the options <u>carefully</u>.

> **Example:** Describe the tonality at the end of this extract. Circle your answer.
>
> atonal　　major　　minor　　pentatonic

If you get stuck, <u>guess</u> the answer — there's a <u>25% chance</u> of getting it right. These questions are only worth <u>one mark</u>, but they're quite <u>easy</u> marks to pick up.

2 You'll get some <u>short-answer</u> questions, where you <u>don't</u> need to write <u>full sentences</u>.

> **Example:** Fully describe the interval between the first two notes of the melody. *(2 marks)*

Check how many <u>marks</u> are <u>available</u> — if it's a <u>2 mark question</u>, a <u>one-word answer</u> will probably only get you <u>one mark</u>. E.g. make sure you describe intervals <u>fully</u> — put 'major 3rd', not just '3rd'.

3 There are questions where you have to write a <u>longer</u> answer with more <u>detail</u>. They're worth <u>4</u> or <u>5 marks</u>.

> **Example:** How have the timbre and dynamics changed in the second version? *(4 marks)*

Make sure you make <u>four</u> or <u>five good points</u> to get all the <u>marks</u> available.

4 You could get an <u>outline</u> of part of the music called a '<u>skeleton score</u>'. It will just show <u>part</u> of the music with some notation missing. You'll have to fill in the <u>pitch</u>, <u>rhythm</u> or <u>ornamentation</u> of a short section.

> **Example:**  Fill in the missing notes in bar 4 using the given rhythm.

There'll probably be <u>one mark</u> for <u>each thing</u> you have to fill in. So if there are <u>5</u> missing notes, it'll be a <u>5 mark question</u>.

Shiver me timbers — 'tis the skeleton score...

The best way to <u>prepare</u> for this exam is to <u>practise</u>. When you're listening to music, try and pick out things like <u>tempo changes</u>, <u>dynamics</u>, <u>tonality</u>, etc. — and try and work out what <u>time signature</u> it's in.

Composing and Appraising Music

If you thought composing was just about writing the first thing that comes into your head, you're sorely mistaken. There's much more to it than that — like appraising your composition.

First you have to Compose a piece...

1) Unit 2 is called 'Composing and Appraising Music' — it's worth 20% of your total mark.

2) It's divided into two sections — you have to compose one piece of music, and then appraise it. Each section's worth 10%, and there are 20 marks available for each bit.

3) Your composition can be any length, and must cover two or more of the Areas of Study (see p.1). You choose which of the areas you want to look at.

4) The composition also has to be linked to one of the three strands of learning (the Western Classical Tradition, Popular Music of the 20th and 21st Centuries or World Music). The exam board will decide which one you have to focus on — it changes each year, so ask your teacher which one you're doing.

Make sure your piece is long enough to develop some musical ideas.

5) You have up to 20 hours to do your composition, which should be supervised by your teacher.

6) You have to submit two versions of your composition — a recording and a score. The recording can be of live performers, or you can use ICT (or a combination of both). Your score can be in any appropriate format — e.g. standard notation, graphic notation, guitar tabs or a written account (or a combination of these). The recording should closely match the score.

7) To get good marks in this section, your piece must:

- be imaginative and creative
- have a clear, balanced structure
- show development of ideas
- fulfil its intention (see next page)
- be suitable for the instruments it's written for
- include suitable performance directions and dynamics

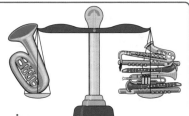

... then you have to Appraise it

1) The appraisal is a written account of your composition.

2) You have 2 hours to do your appraisal under controlled conditions (a bit like an exam).

3) It should be done in an appraisal booklet, which will be provided by the exam board.

4) You'll have to answer questions on your composition — for example:

- Say which AoS you were aiming to cover and why, and say how your piece does this.
- Describe the process of composition.
- Describe any problems you came across, and how you solved them.
- Say how successful your piece is in relation to the AoS and strand you were focusing on.
- Describe the recording process.
- Think about how the piece is linked to its context.

I bet Mozart never had to write an appraisal...

Make sure you think about the Areas of Study you've chosen (and the strand that's been chosen for you) while you're composing your piece. If you don't, it won't meet the requirements, and you'll get lower marks.

Composing and Appraising Music

There's lots of things you have to <u>think</u> about when you're composing — like if you're writing for a particular <u>event</u>, or if your music has a specific <u>purpose</u>. You need to bear in mind <u>who</u> will play it as well.

You have to think about the <u>Audience</u>

1) For this composition, you have to consider the <u>intention</u> of your piece — <u>why</u> you're writing it (the examiners need a better reason than 'because my teacher told me to'...).

2) Think about what your piece will be <u>used for</u> — e.g. to <u>dance</u> to, part of a <u>concert</u>, <u>film music</u>, etc.

3) You also need to decide on the <u>purpose</u> of your piece. This is what you want it to <u>do</u>, e.g. <u>grab attention</u>, <u>set the scene</u>, <u>accompany the action</u> in a play, etc.

Someone might <u>Ask you to write a Specific Piece</u>

1) Sometimes composers are <u>commissioned</u> to write a piece of music — someone will <u>request</u> a piece that they want writing. For example, you could be asked to write a <u>fanfare</u> to open a village fête, or a <u>song</u> to be performed in a school play.

2) If you're working on commission, you have to make sure your piece is <u>exactly what the person wants</u> — you <u>can't</u> just do what <u>you</u> want.

3) Some composers have a <u>patron</u> — almost like a <u>sponsor</u>, who supports them <u>financially</u>. <u>Patronage</u> was more common a few hundred years ago — for example, the 18th century composer <u>Haydn</u> was under the patronage of the wealthy <u>Esterházy</u> family.

Think about the <u>Technical Demands of your piece</u>

1) When you're composing, you have to think about the <u>ability</u> of the players who will perform your piece, and not make it <u>too hard</u> for them. For example, if the only clarinet player in the band is just a <u>beginner</u>, it's no good writing a really <u>tricky</u> clarinet part.

2) You also have to think about what <u>instruments</u> you're writing for, and what they're <u>capable</u> of. For example, you shouldn't write parts that are <u>too high</u> or <u>too low</u> for the instruments, and you have to remember things like giving <u>wind</u> players chances to <u>breathe</u>.

3) If your composition is going to be performed by <u>professional musicians</u> (people who get <u>paid</u> for playing music), then you can make it <u>harder</u> than if you're using <u>amateurs</u> (people who do it for <u>fun</u>).

4) Think about the <u>emotional demands</u> too — e.g. if it's a <u>sad</u> piece, you want to write melodies that the players can put some <u>feeling</u> into. You should provide some <u>directions</u> to the players on how to do this — e.g. by writing <u>instructions</u> about the <u>mood</u> of the piece (*dolce, risoluto*, etc.).

Make sure there's <u>Time to Practise</u>

1) If your piece is going to be performed by a <u>live band</u>, make sure they have time to <u>practise</u> — you can't expect them to <u>sight-read</u> it <u>perfectly</u> on the day of the recording. You should be there at the rehearsals to <u>supervise</u> — you can even play yourself.

2) Remember, other people's <u>interpretation</u> of a piece might be a bit <u>different</u> to yours, so make sure all the <u>musical directions</u> are <u>clear</u>. Otherwise it might not turn out the way <u>you want it</u>.

3) If you've given players room to <u>improvise</u> (see p.21), it'll probably be <u>different</u> every time they play it. Make sure you give <u>clear instructions</u> on what you want it to sound like.

Turning up to rehearsals — that's far too demanding...

Make sure your instructions are <u>clear</u> — I once <u>forgot</u> to include performance directions and the piece was a <u>disaster</u>. The <u>brass</u> section went <u>too fast</u>, the <u>flutes</u> went <u>too slow</u>, and the <u>clarinets</u> didn't even <u>turn up</u>.

Composing and Appraising Music

You also have to think about the <u>occasion</u> you're writing for — including the <u>time</u> and the <u>place</u> your piece will be performed, and <u>who's</u> going to be listening to it.

Music can be Sacred or Secular

1) <u>Sacred</u> music is <u>religious</u> — it's written about <u>religious themes</u>, and often performed in <u>churches</u>. <u>Masses</u>, <u>oratorios</u> and <u>hymns</u> are all examples of sacred music.

2) <u>Secular</u> music is <u>non-religious</u> — it includes things like <u>operas</u> and <u>musicals</u>.

3) <u>Utility</u> music is music written for a <u>specific purpose</u> — e.g. for a particular <u>social event</u>, or for a purpose like <u>dancing</u>.

Music can be Performed in Different Places

1) You need to think about <u>where</u> your piece is going to be performed. Some people play music in <u>private</u> — they play for their own <u>enjoyment</u>, and <u>don't</u> perform in public. It's <u>unlikely</u> that your composition will be played in private (as it needs to be <u>assessed</u>).

2) There are lots of different <u>public places</u> where music is performed — this can be anything from <u>busking</u> to a <u>village fair</u> to a massive <u>music festival</u>. Some of these performances will be <u>free</u>.

3) <u>Concerts</u> often have a more <u>formal</u> venue than other public performances, and the audience will probably have to <u>pay</u>.

4) Music can be <u>shared</u> using different types of <u>media</u>. <u>Radio stations</u> and <u>TV channels</u> dedicated to music give you access to lots of different music, and they're often <u>free</u>.

5) There's lots of music available to <u>download</u> on the <u>internet</u>. You can put your <u>own</u> music on the internet using <u>social networking sites</u>. This can help it reach a much <u>wider audience</u>.

Think about Performing Conventions

1) There are lots of <u>performing conventions</u> in music, and they're different for different types of music. For example, at a <u>classical</u> music concert, the orchestra would <u>stand up</u> when the conductor walked on stage, the conductor would <u>shake the principal's hand</u>, and the orchestra might play the <u>National Anthem</u>.

2) For your composition, you need to think about things like the <u>layout</u> of your band — e.g. whether to stick with a <u>traditional</u> layout (which varies depending on the instruments you've written for) or choose your own.

3) Think about things like whether <u>soloists</u> should <u>stand up</u> or <u>move to the front</u>, or just stay <u>sitting</u> where they are — and whether it will affect the <u>final recording</u>.

You can Submit a Recording of Live Players or use ICT

1) You need to decide whether you want to make a recording of your composition using <u>live performers</u>, <u>ICT</u>, or a <u>combination</u> of both. This will often come down to things like the <u>availability of players</u> and your <u>access</u> to <u>ICT resources</u>.

2) Think about how you want the piece to <u>sound</u> — if you <u>prefer</u> the sound of live instruments, try and write a piece that can be played by them. If you're <u>interested</u> in music technology, then use it in your composition.

3) Some pieces are made up of a <u>mix</u> of <u>pre-recorded parts</u> and <u>live players</u>.

I only play the didgeridoo in private...

Remember, you've got <u>20 hours</u> to compose this piece — but once it's handed in, you can't just forget about it. Oh no. You have to <u>prepare</u> yourself for the <u>appraisal</u>, so make sure you know your piece <u>inside out</u>.

Performing Music

The better you play, the more marks you get, so pick your pieces carefully and practise hard.
Practise till your fingers bleed and the neighbours beg for mercy.

You have to do Two Performances

Unit 3 — Performing Music is worth a whopping 40% of your total mark. That's more
than any other individual unit, so it's worth making sure you put in lots of practice.
You have to perform two pieces:

1) One of the two pieces has to be an individual performance,
which can be technology-based.
2) The other has to be a group piece. This could be anything from a
duet to playing in a full band, as long as you have an important part
(playing third triangle in a symphony orchestra won't quite cut it, I'm afraid).

Say you play the violin, you could do a solo with piano accompaniment for one performance and play in a string quartet for the other.

You can play a different instrument for each performance, but it might be safest to stick to what you're best at.

The Individual Piece is worth 30 Marks

1) Your individual or technology-based performance should last for no more than 5 minutes.
There are 30 marks available for this piece.

2) An individual performance can be an unaccompanied solo (as long as the piece is meant to be
unaccompanied), an accompanied solo (e.g. a piece with a piano accompaniment) or a piece
with a substantial solo part. You have to play or sing an independent part. Your part will probably
be melodic, though it could be rhythmic if you're playing percussion.

3) For a technology-based performance, you have to use a sequencer or multitrack recorder to create
a performance. You have to manipulate the tracks to create your final piece. It must have at least
three parts, and one (or more) of them should be performed in real or step time.

4) You can perform a composition of your own, but it can't be one you've submitted for Unit 2 or Unit 4.

The Marks are Divided Up into Different Criteria

Your performance is marked on different criteria, depending on the type of performance you're doing.

INDIVIDUAL PERFORMANCE

1) LEVEL OF DEMAND — this is how hard the piece is.
There are a maximum of 3 marks available for this.
Your piece must be harder than Grade 4 to get
all 3 marks.

2) ACCURACY — you can get up to 9 marks for accuracy.
You need to pitch your notes correctly (and in tune),
and play the right rhythms.

3) COMMUNICATION — there are 9 marks available for
communication. To get good marks, you need to play
confidently and convincingly.

4) INTERPRETATION — again, you can get up to 9 marks
for how well you interpret the piece. This is things like
tempo, technique, how expressive your performance is
and how well you play the performance directions.

TECHNOLOGY-BASED PERFORMANCE

1) ACCURACY OF PITCH AND RHYTHM —
you can get up to 6 marks for attention
to details like performance directions and
expression.

2) BALANCE — you can get up to 6 marks
for making sure the parts are balanced.

3) DYNAMICS — there are 6 marks available
for using a range of appropriate dynamics.

4) PANNING — again, you can get up to
6 marks for using panning to produce a
clear recording.

5) STYLE — there are another 6 marks
available for using appropriate effects,
like reverb.

Practice makes perfect...

No doubt people have been going on at you about practising since you were knee-high to a piccolo
(whatever that means). The more my music teachers went on at me about practising, the less I felt
like doing it. I expect you know that you need to do lots of practice. So we'll just leave it there.

Performing Music

As well as your <u>individual performance</u>, you also have to do a <u>group performance</u> — it's supposed to show how well you play in an <u>ensemble</u>.

You need At Least Two Players for the Group Performance

1) For your group performance, you must play in an ensemble made up of <u>at least two live players</u> (including yourself).

I hope this counts as 'two live players'.

2) If you're playing in a <u>big ensemble</u>, your part must be <u>easy to pick out</u>.

3) Your group can be <u>conducted</u>, but not by the teacher who's marking your performance.

4) Your piece has to last for <u>no more than 5 minutes</u> and it's worth <u>30 marks</u>.

You're marked on your Ensemble Skills

Your <u>group performance</u> is marked on <u>four</u> different criteria:

1) LEVEL OF DEMAND — how <u>hard</u> the piece is. You can get the maximum <u>3 marks</u> if your piece is <u>above Grade 4</u> standard. In a group performance, this'll often mean that you have an <u>important role</u> within the ensemble, but it may <u>change</u> throughout the piece.

2) ACCURACY — there are <u>9 marks</u> available for accuracy of <u>pitch</u>, <u>intonation</u> (how in tune you are) and <u>rhythm</u>.

3) COMMUNICATION AND INTERPRETATION — you can get up to <u>9 marks</u> for this. You need to demonstrate things like an <u>understanding</u> of the <u>style</u> of the piece, the <u>performance directions</u> and its <u>technical demands</u>. You should play <u>confidently</u>, and your part should <u>stand out</u> (where appropriate).

4) SENSE OF ENSEMBLE — there are another <u>9 marks</u> available for your sense of ensemble. This is how well you play as <u>part of a group</u> and includes things like <u>balance</u>, <u>timing</u> and <u>tuning</u>. You have to <u>respond</u> well to the rest of the group and overcome any <u>problems</u> that might come up.

Make sure you're Well-Practised

In each performance, you need to show off your 'musicality'. You need to think about things like...

<u>Accuracy of pitch and rhythm</u> — This bit's the easiest. Just <u>learn the notes</u>, play them <u>in time</u> and <u>in tune</u>. Most importantly, <u>keep going</u> — lots of stopping and starting or slowing down for tricky bits will lose you marks. Don't worry about the odd slip because of nerves, but start off <u>well prepared</u>.

<u>Expression</u> — Your performance needs to make the audience <u>feel</u> something. Pay attention to stuff like <u>dynamics</u>, <u>tempo</u>, <u>mood</u>, <u>articulation</u> and <u>phrasing</u>. If they're not written in, work out your own.

<u>Interpretation</u> — Use <u>expression</u> and playing techniques that fit the <u>style</u> of your piece — e.g. don't play a lullaby on a distorted electric guitar.

<u>Ensemble skills</u> — Obviously you only get marks for this when you're playing in an ensemble. Play <u>in time</u> with the other players. Really <u>listen</u> to the other parts, so you know when you should be <u>part of the background</u> and when you should make your part <u>stand out</u>. <u>Tune up</u> before you start and listen carefully to <u>intonation</u> (<u>tuning</u>) all the way through.

There's nothing worse than an out-of-tune bagpipe group...

Make sure you choose your pieces <u>carefully</u> — it's no good picking a really <u>tricky</u> piece just to get marks for <u>difficulty</u> if you <u>can't</u> actually play it. On the other hand, if you pick something <u>too easy</u>, you'll be <u>throwing away</u> difficulty marks. Have a word with your music or instrument <u>teacher</u> and get their <u>advice</u>.

Composing Music

You have to do <u>another</u> composition for GCSE Music — and it <u>can't</u> be the same as the one you did for Unit 2. Which is a <u>shame</u>, because it would save you a lot of work. Never mind, eh...

You have 25 Hours to Compose your piece

1) <u>Unit 4 — Composing Music</u> is worth <u>20%</u> of your total marks. There are <u>30 marks</u> available for this composition.

2) You have <u>25 hours</u> of <u>supervised time</u> to write your piece, but you're allowed <u>extra time</u> to do the <u>recording</u> if you need it. You can also do <u>research</u> at home.

3) The piece has to explore <u>at least two</u> of the five <u>Areas of Study</u>, but it can be in <u>any style</u> you like.

4) There's <u>no limit</u> for how long your composition should be. Just make sure it's long enough to show that you've <u>developed</u> some of your <u>ideas</u>.

5) You have to hand in a <u>recording</u> of your piece as well as a <u>score</u>. The recording can use <u>live performers</u>, <u>ICT</u> or a <u>mix</u> of both. The score can be <u>any format</u> that's <u>appropriate</u> for your piece — e.g. <u>standard notation</u>, <u>graphic notation</u>, <u>guitar tabs</u> or a <u>written account</u> of your piece (or a <u>combination</u> of these). The recording should <u>closely match</u> the score.

6) You also have to fill in a <u>Candidate Record Form</u> — this is where you have to say which <u>AoS</u> you're using.

Your Score must be Clear and Detailed

1) You need to produce a <u>clear</u>, <u>accurate score</u>. You'll <u>lose marks</u> if the score and recording are <u>inconsistent</u> — that is, if your score doesn't <u>match</u> the <u>recording</u>.

2) Make sure you include lots of <u>performance directions</u> — things like <u>tempo markings</u>, <u>dynamics</u> and <u>articulation</u>. They must be <u>appropriate</u> to your piece though — don't just put in anything. Think about the <u>style</u> you're writing in.

3) Although you won't be marked on <u>presentation</u>, you might lose marks if the examiners <u>can't follow it</u>.

4) Make sure you don't <u>miss anything out</u> either — if it's in the <u>recording</u>, check that it's in the <u>score</u>.

Your composition will be marked on Six Main Areas

There are <u>six</u> main things you need to think about when you're composing your piece:

- using sounds in <u>imaginative</u> ways
- a <u>clear</u>, <u>balanced structure</u>
- well-developed musical <u>ideas</u>
- awareness of <u>style</u>
- use of <u>appropriate instruments</u>
- appropriate use of musical <u>techniques</u> and <u>devices</u>

imagination ☐
balance ☐
ideas ☐
style ☑
instruments ☐
techniques ☐
& devices

These are covered in more detail on the next page.

What's the score...

It's worth spending a bit of <u>time</u> and <u>effort</u> on your score — don't leave it until the last minute and just scrawl something down. A nice, neat score is much <u>easier to follow</u>, and the examiners will appreciate it. Otherwise, if they're having a <u>bad day</u> and have to mark a <u>messy score</u>, they might curl up in a corner and <u>cry</u>.

Composing Music

There are lots of ways to make your piece sound <u>interesting</u> — and I've very kindly described some of these for you on the page below... Make sure you bear them in mind when you're <u>composing</u>.

To get Top Marks, think about these Six things...

① SOUNDS USED IN IMAGINATIVE WAYS

- Once you've picked your instruments, think carefully about how they can make <u>interesting</u> and <u>contrasting</u> sounds — e.g. pizzicato bits for strings or muted bits for brass instruments.
- Think about how you can use your <u>performance space</u> — e.g. put your performers on two different sides of a stage to give a stereo effect.
- Try out different <u>combinations</u> of instruments — some that you wouldn't usually put together can produce a really interesting sound.

② MUSICAL BALANCE

- Organise your music with a <u>clear</u>, <u>balanced structure</u> (see Section 5 in the Core Book). For example, you might choose to write a piece in <u>ternary</u> form, or you could write a <u>rondo</u>.
- Make sure the <u>parts</u> are balanced too — e.g. if you have <u>one flute</u> and <u>six trumpets</u>, the poor little flute will be <u>drowned out</u>.

③ WELL-DEVELOPED MUSICAL IDEAS

- Don't just use a good idea once and then forget about it. <u>Build up</u> and <u>develop</u> the <u>good bits</u> — e.g. by changing the rhythm from short notes to long notes, or the tonality from major to minor.
- You can even use some ideas <u>again</u> and <u>again</u> — e.g. in a rondo. <u>Theme and variation form</u> builds on the <u>same idea</u>.
- Make sure you have a <u>range</u> of <u>creative ideas</u> — don't just stick with one.

④ AWARENESS OF STYLE

- <u>Listen</u> to lots of music from the <u>style</u> you're composing in.
- Make your piece sound like 'the real thing' by using <u>similar musical ideas</u> — e.g. in a reggae song use offbeat swung quavers, syncopated bass lines and muted guitar sounds.
- Include <u>appropriate performance directions</u> — e.g. it's no good marking a piece *legato* if it's a hard rock piece.

⑤ USE OF INSTRUMENTS

- It sounds <u>obvious</u>, but <u>don't</u> write a part that an instrument <u>can't play</u>.
- You should think about things like how <u>high</u> and <u>low</u> an instrument can play.
- Consider different <u>techniques</u> for different instruments — e.g. tonguing for brass and wind instruments.
- Remember your players' <u>limitations</u> — e.g. oboists need space to breathe and beginners don't have a very good range.

⑥ MUSICAL TECHNIQUES AND DEVICES

- <u>Techniques</u> and <u>devices</u> are those <u>clever tricks</u> composers have used for centuries.
- These include things like <u>imitation</u> and <u>inversion</u> — see Section 6 in the Core Book for loads of examples.

Blimey — I think I need a break after all that...

Gosh, there's a lot on this page. But don't panic — a lot of it you'd do <u>automatically</u>, <u>without</u> really thinking about it. You can just use this page as a <u>checklist</u> when you've finished your composition if you want.

Rhythm

Metre is a unit of measurement — it's the same as 100 cm. Oh no, sorry, this isn't a Maths book, it's a Music book. In which case, metre has an entirely different meaning. See below...

The Time Signature is how many Beats there are in a Bar

1) The time signature is made up of two numbers. The top number tells you how many beats there are per bar, and the bottom number tells you how long the beats are. For example:

3 **4**	This means that there are 3 crotchet beats in every bar.	
2 **2**	This means that there are 2 minim beats in every bar.	
6 **8**	This means that there are 6 quaver beats in every bar.	

2) The tempo is how fast a piece is. You're told what the tempo is at the start of a piece:

> • the tempo might be described by a word (e.g. *moderato*, which means moderately).
> • you might be given a tempo marking (e.g. ♩ = 100, which means 100 crotchet beats a minute). This is sometimes called a metronome marking.
> • if a piece is marked *rubato*, it means you can speed some bits up and slow others down (*rubato* means 'robbed time').

♩ = 60

3) The speed and the pattern of the beats (see below) give the music its pulse — a bit like a heartbeat.

The Pattern the Beats make is called the Metre

Metre can be described as regular, irregular or free, depending on the piece.

REGULAR METRE

1) Regular metre has the same pattern of beats all the way through the piece — every beat in each bar is the same length.
2) The time signature is either simple (it has 2, 3 or 4 as the top number) or compound (it has 6, 9 or 12 as the top number).

> ⇦ See Section 2 of the Core Book for more on this.

3) Music in regular metre with two equal beats in a bar is known as duple metre, music with three equal beats in a bar is called triple metre and music with four equal beats in a bar is in quadruple metre.

IRREGULAR METRE

In pieces with an irregular metre, the beats are grouped together in a different way. The time signature will have a number like 5, 7, 10 or 11 as the top number, and the notes are grouped into twos, threes or fours. For example:

$\frac{5}{8}$ = ♩♩♩♩♩   ⇦   Here, the first beat is a crotchet and the second beat is a dotted crotchet. You'd count it 1 & 2 & a.

FREE METRE

Music with no pattern to the beats at all is in free metre. Some pieces in free metre won't have a time signature, because the bars have different numbers of beats in them. Free metre's quite unusual, but it's still worth knowing about.

I'm feeling a bit simple today...

Make sure you know the difference between simple and compound time, and between regular and irregular metre — it's good if you can spot them in the exam. Try and learn some examples of each type as well.

Fancy Rhythms and Metres

Composers have lots of different ways of making their rhythms more <u>interesting</u> — things like <u>syncopation</u>, <u>dotted rhythms</u> and <u>hemiolas</u>. Try and use some of these in your <u>own</u> compositions.

Syncopation *is used a lot in* Jazz

1) <u>Syncopation</u> is where the <u>strong beats</u> are <u>moved away</u> from the <u>first</u> beat of the bar on to a <u>weaker</u> beat. This gives a lively, <u>off-beat</u> sound.
2) Syncopation can be achieved by <u>shifting</u> the notes around so the <u>strong beats</u> of the tune fall on the <u>off-beats</u>, or by adding <u>accents</u> on the <u>off-beats</u>.
3) <u>Jazz musicians</u> use lots of syncopation to <u>vary</u> their melodies — it makes the tunes more <u>interesting</u>.
4) The <u>guitar riff</u> of '<u>I Can't Get No Satisfaction</u>' by the Rolling Stones is a good example of syncopation.

Triplets *help make music* Syncopated

- A <u>triplet</u> is <u>three</u> notes played in the space of <u>two</u>, like this:
- Triplets are a good way of making things <u>syncopated</u> — the <u>second</u> and <u>third</u> notes of each triplet are <u>off</u> the main beat.

Dotted Notes *change the* Rhythm

- <u>Dotted rhythms</u> make music sound '<u>swung</u>'.
- A dot after a note <u>increases</u> its length by <u>half</u> its original value, then you <u>add</u> another note to make up the rest of the beat.
- Dotted rhythms can make melodies more <u>interesting</u>.

> Another way to change the rhythm by altering note length is by using <u>augmentation</u> (increasing the note values) or <u>diminution</u> (decreasing the note values). There's more on this in Section 6 of the Core Book.

Baroque *composers used* Hemiolas

1) A <u>hemiola</u> is where <u>2 bars</u> of <u>simple triple time</u> (e.g. $\frac{3}{4}$) are played as if they were <u>3 bars</u> of <u>simple duple time</u> (e.g. $\frac{2}{4}$).
2) Composers from the <u>Baroque</u> period (1600-1750) like <u>Bach</u>, <u>Vivaldi</u> and <u>Handel</u> often used hemiolas in their pieces. Listen out for them in Handel's '<u>Water Music</u>' (this example's from the third suite):

- In bar 14, the <u>emphasis</u> is put on beats <u>1</u> and <u>3</u>. In bar 15 the emphasis is on beat <u>2</u>.
- This makes these bars <u>feel</u> like they're in $\frac{2}{4}$, even though the piece is in $\frac{3}{4}$.
- The hemiola is <u>emphasised</u> by the <u>trill</u> in bar 15.

3) Hemiolas are often used at <u>cadences</u> (see Section 4 of the Core Book).

Triplets, hemiolas — *it's enough to drive you dotty...*

Hemiolas are <u>tricky little devils</u> to get your head round — try and <u>listen</u> to lots of different examples of them so you know what they sound like and can spot them. Make sure you know how to <u>spell</u> 'hemiola' as well.

Fancy Rhythms and Metres

When different rhythms are played at the same time, some of them fit together well,
but some of them don't. Rhythms that don't fit can create interesting and crazy effects.

Different Rhythms can be played at the Same Time

POLYRHYTHMS

1) When two or more rhythms are played at the same time, the music is polyrhythmic.
2) The rhythms will often have accents in different places, but still feel as though they fit together.
3) Lots of African music is polyrhythmic.

BI-RHYTHMS

1) Time signatures can be split up into different patterns of beats. For example, $\frac{3}{4}$ can be divided into 3 groups of two quavers or 2 groups of three quavers.

2) In a similar way, $\frac{4}{4}$ can be divided into 4 groups of two quavers or 2 groups of three quavers and one of two quavers.

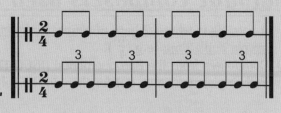

3) These are known as bi-rhythms.

CROSS-RHYTHMS

1) Cross-rhythms are when two or more rhythms that don't fit together are played at the same time, e.g. when triplets are played in one part and normal quavers in another.
2) Cross-rhythms create tension in music.
3) Most percussive music will use some cross-rhythms, and they're used a lot in African music.

Drum Fills are Little Drum Solos

1) Drum fills are fairly short — they often only last for a few beats.
2) Fills are normally used to build the music up, or to change between sections.
3) They give the drummer a (very short) chance to show off.
4) Most rock, pop and jazz pieces will have drum fills in them.

There's a cheeky little drum fill between the first and second verses in 'She Loves You' by the Beatles.

Bert was ready for his big solo

Rhythms make me very cross...

Learn the differences between polyrhythms, bi-rhythms and cross-rhythms, and try not to get them confused.
Listen out for them in African music — you could even include some in your own compositions.

Harmony

Harmony is when <u>two or more</u> notes of <u>different pitch</u> are played at the <u>same time</u>.
The <u>accompanying</u> parts in a piece of music are sometimes called the harmony.

Harmony can be Diatonic or Chromatic

> DIATONIC harmony is when the notes <u>belong</u> to the <u>main key</u> of the piece.

> CHROMATIC harmony is when the notes <u>don't</u> belong to the main key of the piece.

The Difference between two notes is called an Interval

Within an <u>octave</u>, the intervals are:

2nd   3rd   4th   5th   6th   7th   octave

These intervals all start on C, but you can have any note at the bottom.

See Sections 3 & 4 in the Core Book for more on intervals and chords.

When <u>three or more</u> notes are played at the <u>same time</u>, they form a <u>chord</u>. Chords can be <u>major</u> or <u>minor</u>, and can also be <u>dissonant</u> (see below).

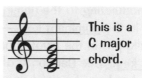

This is a C major chord.

Intervals and Chords are Consonant or Dissonant

CONSONANCE

1) <u>Consonance</u> is a word used to describe <u>chords</u> and <u>intervals</u> that sound <u>nice</u> — the notes sound as if they <u>fit together</u>.
2) <u>3rds</u>, <u>4ths</u>, <u>5ths</u>, <u>6ths</u> and <u>octaves</u> are all consonant. 4ths and 5ths are known as <u>perfect intervals</u>.

Chords that sound nice are sometimes called <u>concords</u>.

DISSONANCE

1) <u>Dissonance</u> is a word used to describe <u>chords</u> and <u>intervals</u> that <u>clash</u> — they don't sound very nice and you want them to <u>resolve</u> (move to a non-clashing note).
2) <u>2nds</u> and <u>7ths</u> are dissonant intervals.
3) Dissonance can be <u>useful</u> if you want to create a sense of <u>terror</u> or build up <u>tension</u>. It's also very useful for <u>modulations</u> (<u>key changes</u>).

Chords that clash are also called <u>discords</u>.

Drones and Pedal Notes add Harmonic Interest

1) A <u>drone</u> is a <u>long</u>, <u>held-on note</u>, usually in the <u>bass</u>.
2) Drones are used a lot in <u>Indian music</u> — they create a <u>foundation</u> that the scale or mode is <u>based on</u>.
3) <u>Pedal notes</u> are a bit different — they're <u>repeated</u> notes, again usually in the <u>bass part</u>. However, the <u>harmony</u> on top of a pedal note <u>changes</u> (whereas a drone sets up the harmony for the whole piece).

Another consonant please...

Ooo, quite a few definitions to learn on this page — make sure you don't get them mixed up. Try not to get <u>concords</u> muddled up with <u>Concorde</u>, the supersonic jet either — they're quite different. <u>Chords</u> and <u>intervals</u> and stuff are covered in more detail in the <u>Core Book</u>, so if you're struggling a bit, have a look in there.

Modulation and Cadences

Key changes in music are common, but they're not just random choices. They usually move to a related key, often the dominant, and the key change is set up by using certain chords.

Key Changes make a piece More Interesting

1) Changing key is known as modulation. It's one way of developing a piece of music, and taking it in new directions. There's more on modulation in Section 4 of the Core Book.
2) A common modulation is to the dominant key — chord V (see Section 3 of the Core Book). So in C major, you would modulate to G major.
3) The dominant key is the same whether you start out in a major or minor key, as chord V is major in both major and minor scales. So in C minor, you would still modulate to G major.
4) The Circle of Fifths (see Section 3 of the Core Book) can help you work out which key to modulate to.

> Another common modulation is to the relative major or minor.

Modulations usually use a Pivot Chord

1) When you're modulating to a new key, you need to find a chord that's the same in both the old key (the tonic) and the new key. This is called the pivot chord.
2) If you're modulating to the dominant key, chord V in the tonic key is the same as chord I in the dominant key — this is a good chord to use as a pivot.
3) You normally put in the pivot chord before a perfect cadence (chord V to chord I) in the new key. See Section 4 of the Core Book for more on cadences.
4) The same chord can be used as a pivot whether you're modulating from a major or minor key. The examples below show how you can modulate from C major to G major and from C minor to G minor using the same pivot chord (the chord of G major).

For example:

Chord V of
C major = Chord I of
G major

Some Minor pieces Finish with a Tierce de Picardie

1) If a piece of music is in a minor key, you'd expect it to finish with a minor chord.
2) However, some composers (especially Baroque composers) choose to finish a minor piece with a major chord, by using a major third in the last chord. This is known as a Tierce de Picardie.

This extract is from Scarlatti's Piano Sonata in G Minor (Cat's Fugue). Even though the piece is in G minor, it finishes with a G major chord.

A major — I'd rather be a Colonel...

Try and fit a modulation into one (or both) of your compositions — but make sure you set it up it properly. It's also useful if you can spot them when you're listening to pieces as well — so get practising.

Revision Summary — Sections 2 & 3

Well, how about that — two Areas of Study out the way in no time at all. There's just time for a few little revision questions before you discover the joy that is Texture and Melody. Make sure you can answer all these questions before you move on — if there's any that you struggle with, go back and read that section again.

1) What does the tempo marking tell you?
2) What does *rubato* mean?
3) What does the top number in the time signature tell you?
4) What does the bottom number in the time signature tell you?
5) Describe regular metre.
6) Is ⅞ regular or irregular metre? Explain your answer.
7) What is free metre?
8) How many centimetres are there in a metre?
9) Describe syncopation.
10) What is a triplet?
11) What does a dot after a note do?
12) Explain what a hemiola is.
13) Name three composers who used hemiolas.
14) Describe   a)   polyrhythms,
             b)   bi-rhythms,
             c)   cross-rhythms.
15) What sort of music often uses polyrhythms and cross-rhythms?
16) What's a drum fill?
17) Describe   a)   diatonic harmony,
             b)   chromatic harmony.
18) Explain what's meant by consonance.
19) Give three examples of consonant intervals.
20) What is dissonance?
21) What's a drone?
22) What type of music uses a lot of drones?
23) Describe a pedal note.
24) What is modulation?
25) What is the dominant of C major?
26) What's a pivot chord?
27) Explain what a Tierce de Picardie is.
28) If a piece is in F minor and finished with a Tierce de Picardie, what's the final chord?

Texture

When there's one part, the music's pure and simple, but put lots of parts together and it's much more complex.

Texture is How the parts Fit Together

1) An important part of music is how the different parts are woven together. This is known as texture — it describes how the melody and accompaniment parts fit together.

2) Monophonic, homophonic and polyphonic are all different types of texture — see Section 4 of the Core Book for more about them.

3) Some textures are made up of the same melodic line that's passed round different parts. Imitation and canons are good examples of this.

Imitation — repeat a phrase with Slight Changes

original phrase   *original phrase, one octave higher*

imitation with modulation   *overlap starts in relative minor*

1) In imitation a phrase is repeated with slight changes each time.

2) It works particularly well if one instrument or voice imitates another and then overlaps.

In a Canon, the Same Melody is played in Different Parts

1) In a canon, each part plays the same melody, but they come in separately and at regular intervals. The parts overlap.

2) A canon is also known as a round. There are some really well-known rounds, e.g. 'London's Burning'.

3) Canons are an example of contrapuntal (or polyphonic) music (see Section 4 of the Core Book).

4) Composers from the Baroque period (1600-1750) like Bach and Vivaldi used lots of canons.

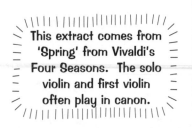

This extract comes from 'Spring' from Vivaldi's Four Seasons. The solo violin and first violin often play in canon.

Solo Violin

First Violin

Solo Violin

First Violin

Looping and Layering are Modern Techniques

1) In the 1960s and 70s, composers like Steve Reich started developing new techniques in their music.

2) They took recordings of sections of music, words, rhythms and other sounds and repeated them over and over again. These are called loops.

3) The loops were often created by cutting pieces of tape and sticking the ends together so they could be played over and over again — this is looping.

4) If there are lots of different loops being played at the same time it's called layering.

A layer of fruit, a layer of sponge, a layer of custard...

In imitation, the same phrase is repeated with slight changes each time. In ImItAtIOn, thE sAmE phrAsE Is rEpEAtEd wIth slIght chAngEs EAch tImE. Inimitationthesamephraseisrepeatedwithslightchangeseachtime.

Texture

Composers can use <u>different textures</u> to <u>vary</u> their music. They can change the <u>number</u> of instruments and whether they play the <u>same notes</u> or in <u>harmony</u>. They can also <u>split</u> the tune between <u>different instruments</u>.

More Than One Part can play the Same Melody

1) If there's just <u>one part</u> playing with <u>no accompaniment</u>, there's just a <u>single melody line</u>.

2) If there's <u>more than one</u> instrument playing the <u>same melody</u> at the <u>same pitch</u>, they're playing in <u>unison</u>.

3) If there's <u>more than one</u> instrument playing the <u>same notes</u> but in <u>different ranges</u>, they're playing in <u>octaves</u>.

The examples on this page use the melody from Handel's 'Water Music'.

Some instruments play Accompanying Parts

1) The instruments that <u>aren't</u> playing the tune play the <u>accompaniment</u>. Different <u>types</u> of accompaniment give different <u>textures</u>.

There's more on the different textures in Section 4 of the Core Book.

2) If the accompaniment is playing <u>chords</u> underneath the melody (or the <u>same rhythm</u> of the melody but <u>different notes</u>), the texture is <u>homophonic</u>. It sounds <u>richer</u> than a single melody line, unison or octaves.

3) If there are <u>two choirs</u> singing at <u>different times</u>, the music is <u>antiphonal</u>. The two choirs will often sing <u>alternate phrases</u> — like <u>question and answer</u> or <u>call and response</u>. A lot of <u>early religious vocal music</u> was antiphonal. You can also get the same effect with two groups of <u>instruments</u>.

4) If there's <u>more than one</u> part playing <u>different melodies</u> at the <u>same time</u>, the music is <u>contrapuntal</u> (or <u>polyphonic</u>). Contrapuntal parts <u>fit together</u> harmonically.

Would you care to accompany me to the cinema...

Quite a few tricky <u>textures</u> to learn on this page — and it's important that you don't get them <u>muddled up</u>. Listen to the different types, and try and <u>recognise</u> what they sound like in case they come up in the <u>exam</u>.

Section Four — AoS3: Texture and Melody

Melody

You need a few good <u>technical</u> words to describe <u>melodies</u> — like <u>conjunct</u>, <u>disjunct</u>, <u>triadic</u> or <u>scalic</u>. "But I don't know what they mean," I hear you cry. Aha, that's where this page comes in <u>very handy</u>.

Melodies can be Conjunct or Disjunct

1) <u>Conjunct</u> melodies move mainly by <u>step</u> — notes that are a <u>major 2nd</u> (a <u>tone</u>) apart.
2) The melody <u>doesn't</u> jump around, so it sounds quite <u>smooth</u>. This example shows a conjunct melody:

This extract's from 'The Silver Swan' by Orlando Gibbons.

3) <u>Disjunct</u> melodies move using a lot of <u>jumps</u> — notes that are more than a <u>major 2nd</u> (a <u>tone</u>) apart.
4) The melody sounds quite <u>spiky</u> as it jumps around a lot.
5) Disjunct melodies are <u>harder</u> to sing or play than conjunct ones. This example shows a disjunct melody:

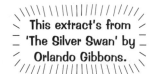

This one's from 'Nessun Dorma' by Puccini.

Triadic Melodies use the notes of a Triad

1) Triads are chords made up of <u>two intervals</u> of a third on top of each other — so triadic melodies usually move between the notes of a triad. (There's more on triads in Section 4 of the Core Book.)
2) For example, a <u>C major</u> triad is made up of the notes <u>C</u>, <u>E</u> and <u>G</u>. There's a <u>major third</u> between C and E, a <u>minor third</u> between E and G and a <u>perfect fifth</u> between <u>C</u> and <u>G</u>. There's more on intervals in Section 3 of the Core Book.
3) This example shows a triadic melody:

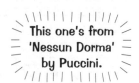

This extract is from the first movement of Haydn's Trumpet Concerto.

Scalic Melodies use the notes of a Scale

1) A <u>scalic</u> melody moves up and down using the notes of a <u>scale</u>.
2) Scalic melodies are <u>similar</u> to conjunct melodies, but they can only move to the <u>next note</u> in the <u>scale</u>. Conjunct melodies can have a few <u>little jumps</u> in them.
3) Like conjunct melodies, scalic melodies sound quite <u>smooth</u>. Here's an example of a scalic melody (it's also from the first movement of Haydn's Trumpet Concerto):

Don't upset the triads...

These different types of melody are pretty <u>easy</u> to spot if you have the <u>music</u> there in front of you, but it's a bit <u>harder</u> if you're <u>listening</u> to them. Listen out for them in all types of music and practise <u>identifying</u> them.

Blue Notes

Like most music, blues gets a lot of its flavour from the scales it uses.

African Slaves in America started off the Blues

1) Blues music started in the 19th century as a type of African American folk song. The earliest blues songs were sung by African slaves working in terrible conditions on plantations in the USA.

2) In the early stuff, a solo singer is accompanied by guitar or banjo and the song lyrics are sad.

3) When the blues hit American cities, singers were backed by jazz instruments like trumpets, clarinets, piano and double bass.

4) In the 1950s and 1960s a style called rhythm'n'blues (R'n'B) was developed. It's played on instruments like the electric guitar and bass.

5) Most blues songs and many pop songs are written to a pattern called the 12-bar blues...

> **12-BAR BLUES**
> * The 12-bar blues pattern's in 4/4 time and 12 bars long.
> * The only chords are I, IV and V.
> * They're used in a set pattern through the 12 bars.
> * The 12-bar structure is repeated all through the song.
> * Minor 7ths are often added to the chords, e.g. C7 — CEGB♭, F7 — FACE♭, and G7 — GBDF. This makes the music sound even more bluesy.

BAR 1	BAR 2	BAR 3	BAR 4
Chord I	Chord I	Chord I	Chord I

BAR 5	BAR 6	BAR 7	BAR 8
Chord IV	Chord IV	Chord I	Chord I

BAR 9	BAR 10	BAR 11	BAR 12
Chord V	Chord IV	Chord I	Chord V
			Chord I

In the very last bar of the song, you play chord I (not chord V).

Blues has its Own Scale

1) You get a blues scale by flattening the third and seventh of any major scale by a semitone. The fifth note's sometimes flattened too.

2) The flattened notes are known as the blue notes.

3) The blue notes are notes that were 'bent' in African singing. The singers would 'slide' up or down to the note, giving it a twang and making it slightly flatter.

4) The second and sixth notes are often left out.

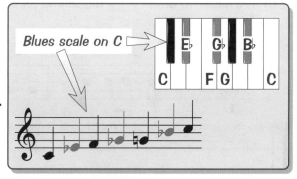

Blues scale on C

Bluesy Bass Lines Turn Up in Lots of Pop Songs

Some blues bass lines are used a lot in pop music. Learn these two so you can spot them:

1) *WALKING BASS* moves in steady one beat notes up and down the notes of chords I, IV and V.

2) *BOOGIE-WOOGIE BASS* is the same notes, played with boogie-woogie rhythm. BB King's 'You Upset Me Baby' has a boogie-woogie bass line.

boo-gie woo-gie

This is one example of a boogie-woogie rhythm.

I feel blue — blue as a blue-blooded bluebird stew...

The blues mainly uses the blues scale, but different types of music use different scales. As well as diatonic scales (major and minor scales, which I bet you're pretty familiar with), there are also chromatic scales, whole tone scales, pentatonic scales and modes. There's more about these in Section 3 of the Core Book.

Ornaments and Expression

To make pieces more <u>exciting</u>, composers put in all sorts of <u>funny little symbols</u> that tell the performer to add <u>fancy bits</u> to the music. It makes it more <u>interesting</u>, both to <u>play</u> and to <u>listen</u> to.

Glissandos and Portamentos are Slides between notes

1) <u>Glissandos</u> and <u>portamentos</u> are when the player or singer <u>starts</u> on one note then <u>slides</u> to another.

2) They're indicated by a <u>straight</u> or <u>wiggly line</u> between two notes.

3) <u>Bent notes</u> are when the player or singer starts a little bit <u>above</u> or <u>below</u> the note then <u>bends</u> to it. They sound a bit like a <u>wobble</u>. The lead guitar in <u>BB King's</u> '<u>You Upset Me Baby</u>' plays lots of bent notes.

4) Other ways of <u>decorating</u> a tune include adding <u>ornaments</u> — e.g. <u>passing notes</u>, <u>appoggiaturas</u>, <u>trills</u>, <u>turns</u> and <u>mordents</u>. There's more about these in Section 2 and Section 4 of the Core Book.

Phrases are like Musical Sentences

1) Music is divided up into <u>phrases</u> — they're a bit like <u>musical sentences</u>.

2) Phrases are often <u>two</u>, <u>four</u> or <u>eight bars</u> long, but can be <u>any length</u>.

3) They're indicated by a <u>curved line</u> above the stave.

4) They help give the music a <u>structure</u> and make it <u>flow better</u>. You usually <u>breathe</u> in <u>between</u> phrases (and <u>not</u> in the <u>middle</u> of them).

5) If the composer <u>hasn't</u> put in phrase marks, it's up to <u>performers</u> to divide the piece up themselves.

6) It's easier to divide <u>vocal</u> music into phrases, as the phrases can follow the <u>lyrics</u> — like in this example from <u>Puccini's</u> '<u>Nessun Dorma</u>':

tu pu- reo prin-ci - pes - sa nel-la tua fred-da stan - za

Take care not to confuse phrase marks with slurs.

Articulation tells you how to Play the Notes

1) Composers use <u>symbols</u> to tell you to play certain notes <u>shorter</u>, <u>longer</u> or with more <u>attack</u> than normal.

2) <u>Short</u> notes are shown with a <u>dot</u> above or below the note — these are <u>staccato</u> notes and should be <u>separated</u> and <u>detached</u> from other notes.

3) <u>Tenuto</u> marks (<u>lines</u> above or below a note) tell you that a note should be held for its <u>full length</u>, or even played slightly <u>longer</u>.

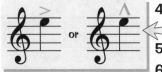

4) Symbols like this > or like this ∧ are <u>accents</u> — you should <u>emphasise</u> these notes or put more of an <u>attack</u> on them.

5) Accents are played on wind and brass instruments by <u>tonguing</u> the note <u>harder</u>.

6) <u>String</u> players have to use their <u>bows</u> to <u>attack</u> accented notes.

7) If <u>all</u> the notes should be accented, the music might be marked <u>marcato</u>.

My friend has a really funny accent...

Music without phrases wouldn't make much sense it would be like having a paragraph with no punctuation you wouldn't know where to breathe and if you tried to play it in one breath you'd just end up in a heap on the floor which wouldn't look very good in the middle of a concert or in your performance exam so it's important

Improvisation

Improvisation isn't just making up whatever you like. There's actually quite a bit more to it.

Lots of Jazz is Improvised

1) Improvisation is where a performer makes up music on the spot. There's often an improvised solo section in jazz pieces.
2) The improvisations aren't totally random though — the soloist will be told which chords to improvise over. This is often a 12-bar blues chord pattern (see p.19). Some improvisations use a mode (see Section 3 of the Core Book) instead of a chord pattern.
3) The soloist will know which notes are in each chord, but sometimes they'll play clashing notes to keep the solo interesting. If they're using a mode, they'll use the notes of the mode in their solo.
4) They might also use bits of the main melody of the piece as a starting point, then develop it into a much more complex phrase.
5) Some performers pinch bits of other tunes in their solos — it keeps the audience entertained when they spot them.
6) Rock songs will often include an improvised guitar solo — like in Led Zeppelin's 'Stairway to Heaven'.

Improvisation uses lots of Different Techniques

1) Performers use lots of different musical ideas and techniques in their solos — it gives them a chance to show off.
2) Improvisations will often be syncopated to make them feel 'jazzy'. Triplets and dotted rhythms can help the tunes flow (see p.11).
3) Ornaments (like passing notes and appoggiaturas) make the tunes more exciting (see Section 2 of the Core Book). Blue notes (see p.19) are often used in jazz improvisations.
4) A wide range of dynamics (see p.27) and accents (see p.20) also help keep the solos interesting.

Oh, sorry, not that type of triplet.

Indian Music uses Improvisation too

1) Improvisation isn't just used in Western music — it's an important part of Indian music as well.
2) The improvisations are based on a raga — a set of notes (usually between 5 and 8) that are combined to create a particular mood. There are hundreds of different ragas. Each one is named after a different time of day or season and is supposed to create an atmosphere like the time or season it's named after.
3) Raga performances are improvised, but based on traditional tunes and rhythms. These are never written down — they're passed on from generation to generation aurally.
4) The improvised melody is often played on an Indian instrument called a sitar (see p.24), but it's sometimes performed by a singer instead. They only use the notes of the raga.
5) The melody is played over a drone — a long held-on note that provides the harmony (see p.13).

These are the notes of the raga vibhasa, a dawn raga. The melody would be improvised using these notes over a drone.

I'll improvise my way through the listening exam...

In all types of improvisation, it's really important that the performer knows their scales (or mode or raga). So even though practising your scales is about as exciting as watching jelly set, it's well worth doing.

Revision Summary — Section 4

Well, that's another section out of the way. This section covers quite a range of stuff, so make sure you've got your head round it. Before you nip off to get yourself a nice cup of tea and a biscuit, there's one little revision summary to do first. If you can answer all these questions without looking back at the pages, you're well on your way to becoming a GCSE Music expert.

1) What is texture?

2) Explain what is meant by imitation.

3) What's a canon?

4) Give another name for a canon.

5) What's a loop?

6) Describe what layering is.

7) Explain how playing in unison is different from playing in octaves.

8) Explain what is meant when music is described as,
      a) homophonic,
      b) antiphonal,
      c) contrapuntal.

9) Give another word for contrapuntal.

10) Explain what is meant by each of the following words that are used to describe melodies:
      a) conjunct,
      b) disjunct,
      c) triadic,
      d) scalic.

11) How did blues music start out?

12) Name two instruments that were played in early blues pieces.

13) Which three chords are used in a 12-bar blues?

14) Write out the chord pattern used in 12-bar blues.

15) Which notes are flattened in a blues scale?

16) What are these flattened notes called?

17) Name and describe two different blues bass lines.

18) Describe what a glissando is.

19) What do phrases do?

20) What effect does a dot above or below a note have?

21) What effect does a line above or below a note have?

22) Draw two different symbols used to show an accent.

23) Name two different types of music that use a lot of improvisation.

24) Name three different things performers can do to keep improvised solos interesting.

25) What is a raga?

World Music Instruments

Drums are an important part of African music, but other instruments are popular too.

Drums Play a Big Part in African Culture

1) Drums are probably the most widely played instrument in Africa.
2) In tribal society, drums get a lot of respect — they're thought of as one of the best instruments.
3) Drums are used to play an accompaniment for singing, dancing and even working.
4) Drums are also used to call people together for important community events like weddings and funerals — a bit like church bells in Europe. There are different drum beats for different events, so people from neighbouring villages can tell what's going on just by listening.
5) Most African drum music is passed on through oral tradition — it's not written down.

These are the Main Types of Drum...

1) The djembe is originally from Guinea and Mali in West Africa. It has a single head and is shaped a bit like a goblet. It's played with the hands. The overall size of the drum affects its pitch — smaller drums are higher-pitched.

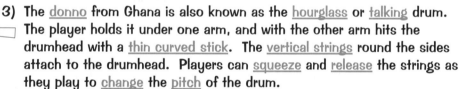

*

not to scale

2) The dundun is played in Guinea and Mali too. Dundun are cylindrical drums played with sticks. There's a drum skin at each end, so they're played horizontally.
There are three types: KENKENI — a high-pitched drum that keeps the pulse going.
SANGBAN — a mid-pitched drum.
DOUNDOUN — a large, low-pitched drum.

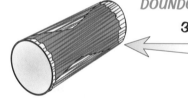

3) The donno from Ghana is also known as the hourglass or talking drum. The player holds it under one arm, and with the other arm hits the drumhead with a thin curved stick. The vertical strings round the sides attach to the drumhead. Players can squeeze and release the strings as they play to change the pitch of the drum.

4) The kagan (a small barrel-shaped drum) and the kidi (a medium-sized barrel drum) are both from Ghana.

The Balophon, Kora and Thumb Piano are Popular

These are some of the most popular instruments apart from drums.

A BALOPHON is a wooden xylophone. The lumpy things hanging under the keys are dried gourds (vegetables a bit like pumpkins). They create a warm, mellow sound.

The KORA is made and played by the Mandingo people. It's got 21 strings and you play it by plucking — a bit like a harp.

The MBIRA or THUMB PIANO is really popular — partly because it's pocket-sized. It makes a liquid, twangy sound.

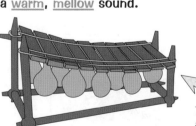

These two are mostly played in West Africa.

The thumb piano is played all over Africa.

My drums are called Nigel and Dave...

Unless you've got a photographic memory, or are otherwise brilliantly gifted with powers of learning far beyond those of us ordinary mortals, you can't just go skipping over the names of the drums and other instruments. Learn them. Learn how to spell them. Learn the facts about them. Learn it all now.

World Music Instruments

You need to know about the main <u>instruments</u> played in traditional <u>Indian</u> music and in <u>salsa</u> music.

The <u>Sitar</u>, <u>Tambura</u> and <u>Tabla</u> are <u>Indian Instruments</u>

1) A <u>sitar</u> is a large, long-necked <u>string</u> instrument.
2) On a seven-string sitar, five of the strings are plucked for the <u>melody</u>, and the other two create <u>drone</u> notes.
3) Sitars also have '<u>sympathetic</u>' strings <u>underneath</u> the <u>main strings</u>. The sympathetic strings <u>vibrate</u> when the main strings are played, creating a <u>thick</u>, <u>shimmery</u> sound.
4) The <u>frets</u> on a sitar can be moved to <u>different positions</u> for <u>different pieces</u>.
5) Sitar players can pull strings to make notes '<u>bend</u>' or <u>distort</u>.
6) Sliding a finger along a string gives a <u>glissando</u> sound (see p.20) called <u>mind</u>.

The <u>tambura's</u> a similar shape to the sitar. It usually has <u>four</u> metal strings, but can have up to <u>six</u>. It's used as more of a <u>backing</u> instrument.

A <u>tabla</u> is a <u>pair</u> of drums. The <u>smaller</u>, right-hand drum is called the <u>tabla</u> (also called the <u>dayan</u>). The <u>larger</u>, lower-sounding drum is called the <u>bayan</u>.

Other instruments used in Indian music include the <u>sarod</u> (an instrument like a small <u>sitar</u> with a <u>fretless</u> fingerboard), the <u>sarangi</u> (a small, <u>bowed</u> stringed instrument with <u>no frets</u>), the <u>bansuri</u> or <u>venu</u> (a <u>flute</u> made of <u>bamboo</u>), the <u>shehnai</u> (an instrument with a <u>double reed</u>, like an oboe) and the <u>harmonium</u> (a <u>keyboard instrument</u> powered with air pumped by hand bellows). <u>Singers</u> sometimes perform as well.

Salsa Music comes from Cuban Son

There are lots of different types of <u>Caribbean music</u> — including <u>Cuban son</u>, <u>Jamaican reggae</u> and <u>Trinidadian calypso</u>. The <u>guiro</u> and <u>maracas</u> (see below) are popular throughout the Caribbean. Caribbean music has <u>European</u> and <u>African influences</u> and can be mixed with other types to create <u>new styles</u> — e.g. <u>salsa</u> is a mix of <u>Cuban son</u> and <u>New York jazz</u>. A <u>modern salsa band</u> combines <u>son</u> and <u>big band</u> instruments:

FRONT LINE or HORNS

<u>Trombones</u>, <u>trumpets</u> or <u>saxophones</u> usually play the tune.

VOCALS

There are <u>soneros</u> (lead singers) and the <u>choro</u> (the chorus).

STRINGS and PIANO

A <u>bass guitar</u>, the <u>Spanish guitar</u> and a <u>piano</u> provide an accompaniment to the brass section.

RHYTHM SECTION

Latin American instruments like <u>congas</u>, <u>timbales</u>, <u>bongos</u>, <u>maracas</u>, a <u>guiro</u>, and a standard <u>drum kit</u> are used.

BONGOS (and other drummish things)
*Bongos are paired drums played with the hands.
Congas and timbales are also paired drums.*

GUIRO
*makes a
scrapy noise*

MARACAS

Can we have a tabla for four please...

Lots more names to learn on this page (sorry about that). See if you can find some <u>recordings</u> of the typical Indian and salsa instruments so you can <u>identify</u> them if they come up in your exam.

Timbre

When you're listening to music, you can pick out individual instruments because of their unique sound
— e.g. a trumpet sounds nothing like a violin. This is all down to a little thing called timbre.

Every Instrument has its own Timbre

1) Timbre is the type of sound that different instruments make. It's also known as tone colour.

2) Musical notes (and all sounds) are made by vibrations. Different instruments produce vibrations in different ways. For example, on a string instrument, the bow is drawn across the string to make it vibrate. On a brass instrument the vibrations are produced when the player 'buzzes' their lips. The different vibrations make the timbres different.

3) The size and material of the instrument alter the timbre as well — e.g. a cello has a different timbre to a violin because it's bigger, and wooden flutes sound different from metal ones.

4) Timbre can be altered by changing the dynamics and articulation.

Instruments from the Same Family have Similar Timbres

Even though each instrument has a unique timbre, it can still sometimes be hard to tell ones from the same family apart. Different families of instruments change the timbre in different ways:

STRING INSTRUMENTS

- String instruments (like the violin, viola, cello and double bass) have a warm sound. Notes are produced by making the strings vibrate, either using a bow or the fingers.
- All string instruments can be played con arco (with a bow), pizzicato (plucked), con sordino (muted) or sul ponticello (close to the bridge).
- Double stopping is when two strings are pressed at the same time, so two notes can be played at once.
- Tremolo is a very fast trill between notes — it sounds like trembling.

PIANO

- When you press the keys, a hammer hits the strings inside the piano, making them vibrate.
- The timbre of the piano can be changed by using the soft or sustain pedals.

There's more on families of instruments and types of ensembles in Section 7 of the Core Book.

WOODWIND INSTRUMENTS

- Wind instruments (e.g. flute, clarinet, oboe and bassoon) have a soft, mellow sound.
- Edge-tone instruments (e.g. flutes) make a softer, breathier sound than reed instruments (e.g. clarinets).
- Clarinets and oboes can alter their timbre by using a technique called 'bells up', where the player points the end of the instrument upwards. This produces a harsher sound.

BRASS INSTRUMENTS

- Brass instruments (like the trumpet, French horn, trombone and tuba) have a bright, metallic sound.
- Playing with a mute (con sordino) can change the timbre.

PERCUSSION INSTRUMENTS

- Percussion instruments (e.g. drums and xylophones) make a sound when they're struck.
- What you hit them with can change the timbre — e.g. whether you use sticks, brushes or your hands.

SINGERS

- Singers produce notes when their vocal chords vibrate.
- The speed that they vibrate changes the pitch and the timbre — e.g. bass voices sound very different to sopranos.
- Techniques like vibrato (making the note wobble) can give a richer sound.
- Falsetto singing produces a much thinner sound.

I'm picking up good vibrations...

...or maybe it's just the wind in the trees. Who knows. What I do know, however, is that you'll need to learn this stuff really well so you can describe the timbre of different instruments that crop up in your exam.

Timbre

Electronic effects can be used to alter the timbre of some instruments.

There are lots of different Guitar Effects

1) There are loads of different ways to change the sound of an electric guitar.
2) These effects are really popular with rock bands, especially during guitar solos.
3) Guitarists use pedals (e.g. a wah-wah pedal) to alter the tone or pitch.
4) They create effects like:

- DISTORTION — distorts the sound.
- REVERB — adds an echo to the sound.
- CHORUS — creates a slightly delayed copy of the original sound and combines the two together, making it sound as if there's more than one player or singer.
- PHASER — creates a 'whooshing' effect (a bit like the noise an aeroplane flying overhead makes).
- FLANGER — similar to a phaser, but makes a more intense sound. It's used a lot in sci-fi programmes.
- PITCH SHIFTING — used to bend the natural note or add another harmony.
- OCTAVE EFFECTS — creates octaves above or below the note being played.

Synthesised Sounds **have** _Different Timbres_ **to** _Real Sounds_

1) The natural sound of an instrument can be digitally reproduced to create a synthesised sound.
2) Electronic keyboards have different settings, so they can be made to sound like pretty much any instrument, from violins to percussion.

> One big difference between real and synthesised sounds is what happens to the timbre when the volume changes. When a real instrument is played louder, it has a different timbre to when it's played quietly. However, a synthesised sound has the same timbre at any volume — it's just the loudness that changes.

Sampling **uses** _Recordings_ **of** _Real Instruments_

1) The most effective way to recreate the sounds of real instruments is to use sampling.
2) Sampling is where you record an instrument and use the recording (called a sample) in your music.
3) The samples can be altered to create different effects — there are lots of different computer programs that help you do this.
4) Samples can be looped (played over and over again — see p.16), and other samples can be added over the top.
5) Most electronic music produced today uses looping, especially drum patterns.
6) It's not just instruments that can be sampled — you can take samples of anything you like, e.g. traffic noises or doorbells.
7) Lots of pop songs use samples — Kanye West sampled Ray Charles' 'I Got A Woman' in his 2005 hit 'Gold Digger'.

Oh great, someone's sampled my drums again...

I'd like a sample of that cake please...

Looping is repeating the same sample over and over again. Looping is repeating the same sample over and over again. Looping is repeating the same sample over and over again. Looping is repeating the same sample...

Dynamics

You'll know lots about <u>dynamics</u> already, so I won't go <u>on and on</u> about them. Composers in <u>different periods</u> used dynamics in <u>different ways</u> though, and you need to know about that too...

Dynamics <u>tell you how</u> Loud <u>or</u> Quiet <u>to play</u>

1) <u>Dynamics</u> vary from <u>pianissimo</u> (very quiet) to <u>fortissimo</u> (very loud). There's a <u>range</u> of <u>volumes</u> in between:

Quietest   Loudest

pp   *p*   *mp*   *mf*   *f*   *ff*

pianissimo   piano   mezzo piano   mezzo forte   forte   fortissimo

There's more on dynamics in Section 2 of the Core Book.

2) A <u>crescendo</u> (written *cresc.* or) tells you to get <u>louder</u>.

3) A <u>diminuendo</u> (written *dim.* or) tells you to get <u>quieter</u>.   These symbols are also called <u>hairpins</u>.

4) A <u>sforzando</u> (written *sf* or *sfz*) is a <u>sudden</u>, <u>loud accent</u>.

The way dynamics are used has <u>Changed</u> over <u>Time</u>

Baroque 1600–1750

1) The <u>Baroque period</u> lasted from about <u>1600-1750</u> and included composers like <u>Handel</u>, <u>Bach</u> and <u>Vivaldi</u>.

2) Baroque music used lots of fancy <u>ornaments</u> and often had a <u>basso continuo</u> (see p.33). Lots of Baroque music was <u>polyphonic</u> (see p.16-17).

3) <u>Dynamics</u> in the Baroque period <u>weren't</u> very <u>varied</u> — the music was either <u>loud</u> or <u>soft</u>. There <u>weren't</u> many <u>gradual changes</u> in volume like <u>crescendos</u> or <u>diminuendos</u>.

4) A popular Baroque instrument was a <u>keyboard instrument</u> called the <u>harpsichord</u>.  They're played by pressing the <u>keys</u>, which causes a <u>lever</u> inside to <u>pluck</u> the <u>strings</u>. You <u>can't change</u> the <u>strength</u> of the pluck, so you can't change the <u>dynamics</u>.

Classical 1750–1820

1) The <u>Classical period</u> was from about <u>1750-1820</u>. <u>Beethoven's</u> early work and music by composers like <u>Haydn</u> and <u>Mozart</u> is Classical.

2) Classical music was very <u>balanced</u>, and had <u>fewer ornaments</u> than Baroque music.

3) The <u>dynamics</u> were more <u>subtle</u> than in Baroque music — composers used <u>crescendos</u> and <u>diminuendos</u> rather than <u>sudden changes</u>.

4) The <u>piano</u> was very popular in the Classical period as it could play a <u>range</u> of <u>dynamics</u> — the <u>harder</u> you hit the key, the <u>harder</u> the hammer strikes the string and the <u>louder</u> the note.

Romantic 1820–1900

1) The <u>Romantic period</u> was from about <u>1820-1900</u>. <u>Beethoven's</u> later work and music by composers like <u>Tchaikovsky</u> and <u>Chopin</u> is Romantic.

2) Romantic music was very <u>dramatic</u> and <u>expressive</u>. Composers used a lot of <u>accents</u> and <u>sforzandos</u>.

3) They also used a <u>wide range</u> of <u>dynamics</u> — from *ppp* to *fff*. There were <u>sudden changes</u> and <u>massive crescendos</u> and <u>diminuendos</u>, which sometimes lasted for the <u>whole piece</u>.

I love Baroque and roll...

Imagine how <u>dull</u> music would be if there weren't any dynamics. It's something to think about when you're writing your own <u>compositions</u> for Units 2 and 4 — don't forget to put dynamic markings in.

Common Structures

Binary, ternary and rondo forms are all really popular. You need to know the key features of each structure.

Music in Binary form has Two Sections

1) Binary means something like 'in two parts' — there are two bits to a tune in binary form.

2) Baroque composers like Bach and Handel used binary form a lot — e.g. the Minuet from the first suite of Handel's Water Music is in binary form.

3) Each section is usually repeated. You play Section A twice, and then Section B twice — so you end up with an AABB structure.

4) Section B contrasts with Section A — the two parts should sound different.

5) The contrast's often made by modulating to related keys. Pieces in a minor key usually modulate to the relative major, e.g. A minor to C major. Pieces in a major key usually modulate to the dominant key (V), e.g. C major to G major. There's more about modulation in Section 4 of the Core Book.

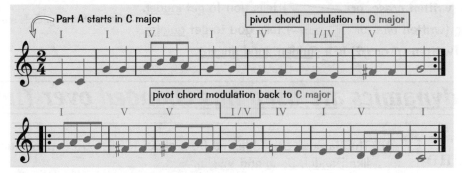

Ternary form has Three Sections

1) Ternary means 'in three parts' — there are three sections in music with ternary form. Often each section is repeated, so it goes AABBAA.

2) Section A ends in the home key, normally with a perfect cadence (see Section 4 in the Core Book). This makes it sound like a complete piece in itself.

3) In Section B the music modulates to a related key, like the dominant or relative minor, and then goes back to the main key before it ends.

  - When the music goes back to A for the last section it can be exactly the same or varied a bit.
  - If this section is varied you call it A1 instead of A.
  - A1 can be different, but not so different that you can't tell it's a variation of A.

Rondo Form can have Any Number of sections

1) Rondo means going round. A rondo starts with a main idea in Section A, moves into a new section, goes round again to A, moves into another new section, goes round again to A... as many times as you like. The new section always contrasts with Section A.

2) Section A is known as the main theme or refrain. The contrasting sections are called episodes.

3) The main theme is always in the main key. Each episode tends to modulate to a related key for contrast.

4) The last movements of many Classical sonatas are in rondo form.

Please refrain from colouring in the cat...

Make sure you can spot all these different forms in case they come up in your Listening Exam.
Rondo form's a particularly nice one — the theme comes back again and again so it's quite easy to identify.

Common Structures

Call and response is used a lot in blues, rock and pop, as well as African and Indian music — so it's dead important that you know what it is. It's used in both instrumental and vocal music.

Call and Response is like a Musical Conversation

1) Call and response is a bit like question and answer. It takes place either between two groups of musicians, or between a leader and the rest of the group.

2) One group (or the leader) plays or sings a short phrase. This is the call. It's then answered by the other group. This is the response.

3) The call ends in a way that makes you feel a response is coming — e.g. it might finish with an imperfect cadence (see Section 4 of the Core Book).

4) Call and response is very popular in pop and blues music. Often the lead singer will sing the call and the backing singers will sing the response.

In a 12-bar blues structure (see p.19), the usual pattern of a call and response would be A, A1, B:

A is the call (4 bars)
A1 is the call repeated with slight variations (4 bars)
B is the response (4 bars).

4 bars	4 bars	4 bars
A — CALL	A1 — CALL WITH VARIATION	B — RESPONSE

To make things more complicated, sections A and B can have a 2-bar call and response of their own:

2 bars	2 bars	2 bars	2 bars	2 bars	2 bars
CALL	RESPONSE	CALL	RESPONSE	CALL	RESPONSE

A — CALL	A1 — CALL WITH VARIATION	B — RESPONSE

Indian and African music use Call and Response

1) In Indian music, call and response is usually used in instrumental music. One musician will play a phrase and it'll either be repeated or improvised upon by another musician.

2) African music uses call and response in religious ceremonies and community events. The leader will sing first and the congregation will respond.

3) Call and response is also used in African drumming music. The master drummer plays a call and the rest of the drummers play an answering phrase.

Some melodies form an Arch Shape

1) If a melody finishes in the same way it started, then the tune has an arch shape.

2) The simplest example of this is ABA — where the first section is also the last section of the piece. This is extended in some pieces to ABCBA, or even ABCDCBA.

3) This gives a symmetrical melody because the sections are mirrored. It makes the whole piece feel more balanced.

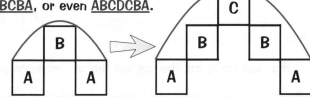

For a banana shape — lie on the floor and arch your back...

Call and response is used in a lot of music — make sure you can spot it in case it comes up in the exam. Take care not to confuse arch-shaped melodies with rondo form — Section A only returns once in an arch.

Theme and Variations

Theme and variation form is exactly what it says it is — a theme, followed by variations on the theme.

Theme and Variation Form varies the melody

1) In theme and variation form, the theme's usually a memorable tune.

2) The theme's played first. There's a short pause before the first variation's played, then another pause before the next variation. Each variation is a self-contained piece of music. There can be as many or as few variations as the composer wants.

3) Each variation should be a recognisable version of the main theme, but different from all the others.

4) Here are some of ways you can vary a tune:

- Add notes to make the tune more complex.
- Remove notes to simplify the tune.
- Change the metre — say, from two beats in a bar to three.
- Add a counter melody — an extra melody over the top of the theme.
- Change the tempo — speed it up or slow it down.
- Change the key or tonality — e.g. from major to minor.
- Change the accompaniment — e.g. a Classical 'Alberti bass' pattern instead of block chords.

Schubert used theme and variation form

1) Schubert's Piano Quintet Op. 114 'The Trout' is a piece of chamber music. The fourth movement's in theme and variation form.

N.B. A piano quintet isn't five pianos — it's a piano and string quartet.

2) The theme comes from a lied by Schubert (a lied is a type of song — see Section 5 of the Core Book) called *Die Forelle* ('The Trout'). There are six variations on it. The theme's first played by the violin, then the piano and the rest of the ensemble play the variations.

3) The first variation adds notes to the theme. This is called ornamentation.

4) In the second variation, the piano plays an echo of the theme after it's played on the viola, with a slightly different rhythm.

5) The piano has a complicated counter melody in the third variation with lots of demi-semiquavers.

6) The fourth variation's in a different key — D minor, while the theme's in D major.

7) In the fifth variation, the note values are changed to give a different rhythm. It's also in a different key (B♭ major). It's played on the cello, so it's lower than the original theme.

8) In the final variation, the original theme comes back, but it's faster. It's back in D major.

There's something fishy about this page...

You can vary a theme in lots of ways. YoU cAn VaRy A tHeMe In LoTs Of DiFfErEnT wAyS. Y cn vry thm n lts f dffrnt wys. You can vary a theme in lots of ways. One could alter an idea using many diverse methods. syaw fo stol ni emeht a yrav nac uoY. Youcanvaryathemeinlotsofdifferentways. Y C V A T I L O D W.

Common Forms

The movements of big works like symphonies, sonatas and concertos often follow set structures — e.g. sonata form, minuet and trio or scherzo and trio.

A piece in Sonata Form has Three Main Sections

The first movement of a symphony, sonata or concerto is usually in sonata form — e.g. Tchaikovsky's Violin Concerto No.1 in D. The last movement sometimes is as well. Sonata form has three main sections:

EXPOSITION	DEVELOPMENT	RECAPITULATION
Themes are "exposed" — heard for the first time.	Themes go through a number of interesting twists and turns.	Themes are "recapped" — played again.

1) The exposition has two contrasting themes. It ends in a different (but related) key to the one it started in.

2) The development keeps the piece interesting — the themes are taken through lots of variations.

3) The recapitulation pulls it all together again — the themes from the exposition are repeated. They're usually changed slightly — e.g. the composer might add ornaments or shorten them a bit.

Pieces in sonata form often start with a short introduction — usually in the dominant key. Composers sometimes use bridge sections between the themes and links between the main sections. They usually add a coda — a short section that's a bit different to the rest of the piece and finishes it off nicely.

See Section 3 in the Core Book for more on related keys.

A Minuet and Trio has Contrasting Sections

1) The third movement of four-movement symphonies and sonatas is often in minuet and trio form.

2) A minuet is a French dance with three beats in a bar.

3) The trio is another minuet in a contrasting but related key — often the dominant or relative minor. It's often written for three instruments (which is why it's called a trio...).

4) After the trio, the first minuet is played again. This is ternary form — ABA (see p.28).

MINUET	TRIO	MINUET

5) Some of the movements of Handel's Water Music are good examples of minuets.

Later works used a Scherzo instead of a Minuet

1) In later symphonies and sonatas, the third movement is often a scherzo and trio instead of a minuet and trio. Beethoven was one of the first composers to use a scherzo in his pieces — the third movement of his Violin Sonata No. 5 in F (often called 'Spring') is a scherzo. In Schubert's Piano Quintet 'The Trout', the third movement is a scherzo and trio.

2) A scherzo and trio is very similar to a minuet and trio — except that a scherzo is faster and more light-hearted. Scherzo means 'joke' in Italian.

3) In a four-movement piece, the scherzo is normally the fastest and most playful.

4) If a symphony or sonata only has three movements, it's usually the scherzo or minuet that's missed out.

Don't worry, I'll be there in a minuet...

You need to learn the names and features of the different sections of each of these forms — and how they relate to each other. Drawing diagrams might help you remember — use different colours for each section.

Common Forms

Strophic form, through-composed form and da capo arias are all popular structures used in songs.
Cyclic form is usually found in large works like symphonies, but it's also used in some big vocal works.

In Strophic Form each Verse has the Same Tune

1) In strophic form, the same section of music is repeated over and over again with virtually no changes.
2) Strophic form is used in Classical, folk, blues and pop music.
3) In strophic songs, the music for each verse is the same, but the lyrics change in every verse.
   Hymns are a good example of this.
4) Strophic form can be thought of like this: A, A1, A2, A3, etc. — the same section is repeated but with
   a small change (the lyrics).
5) The first part of Led Zeppelin's 'Stairway to Heaven' is in strophic form.

In Through-Composed Form Each Verse is Different

1) Through-composed form is the opposite of strophic form — the music changes in every verse.
2) Every verse of lyrics has different music to accompany it, so there's no repetition.
3) Verses can have different melodies, different chords, or both.
4) This form is popular in opera, as the changing music can be used to tell stories.
   Verses sung by different characters can be completely different.
5) A lot of film music is through-composed — the music has to change to reflect
   what's happening on-screen.

Baroque Composers used Ternary Form in Arias

1) An aria is a solo in an opera or oratorio.
2) Arias from the Baroque period (1600-1750) are often in ternary form (see p.28).
   Arias like this are called 'da capo arias'. Handel wrote lots of these.

After repeating Section A and Section B you come
to the instruction da capo al fine. It means "go back
to the beginning and play to where it says fine".
The fine is at the end of Section A.
That's where the piece finishes.

Works in Cyclic Form have a Common Theme

1) Pieces in cyclic form have common themes in all the movements. These themes link the movements together.
2) Big works like sonatas, symphonies and concertos are sometimes in cyclic form.
3) The linking themes vary in different ways. For example, they might be played on different instruments,
   played faster or slower, or played in a different key in different
   movements. You'll still be able to recognise them though.
4) An example of a common theme in a piece in cyclic form is the
   four-note theme of Beethoven's Fifth Symphony. It appears in
   all the movements of the symphony.

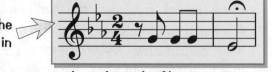

5) Film music often has a theme — a bit of melody that keeps popping up throughout the film.
   The main theme from 'Star Wars®' (by John Williams) is really easy to recognise.

Don't mind me — I'm just passing through...

You might not pay much attention to the music when you're watching a film — but it can make a huge
difference to what you think of a scene or character. Dario Marianelli's music for the film 'Atonement'
and Hans Zimmer's score for the film 'Gladiator' really help set the scene and create tension and emotion.

Common Forms

Continuo and ground bass are both types of bass part. A cadenza is played by a soloist.

A Continuo is a Bass Part

1) A continuo (or basso continuo) is a continuous bass part. Most music written in the Baroque period has a continuo that the harmony of the whole piece is based on.

2) The continuo can be played by more than one instrument, but at least one of the continuo group must be able to play chords (e.g. a harpsichord, organ, lute, harp, etc.). A cello, double bass or bassoon could also be used. The most common combination was a harpsichord and a cello.

3) Continuo parts were usually written using a type of notation called figured bass. Only the bass notes were written on the stave, but numbers underneath the notes told the performers which chords to play. The continuo players would then improvise using the notes of the chord.

4) If there weren't any numbers written, the chord would be a normal triad (the root, the third and the fifth). A 4 meant play a fourth instead of the third, and a 6 meant play a sixth instead of the fifth. A 7 meant that a 7th should be added to the chord.

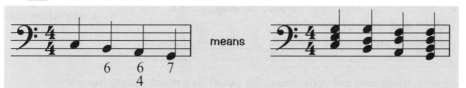

means

> \\\\ ||||||||||| ////
> Some versions of
> Handel's Water Music
> still have the continuo
> written in figured bass.
> //// ||||||||||| \\\\

5) The improvisation is called a realization — the performer would 'realize' a continuo part.

Ground Bass Pieces have Repetition AND Variety

1) A ground bass is a repeated bass part (sometimes called an ostinato) that's usually four or eight bars long. It can be played by the left hand on a harpsichord or piano, or by the cello and double bass in a chamber orchestra.

2) The tune is played over the ground bass part. First you hear the main tune, then a load of variations. The variations are played as one continuous piece — there are no gaps between them.

3) The ground bass part can be varied too. You change the starting note but keep the pattern the same.

First time round, the ground bass tune starts on C. Later on you get the same tune starting on G.

4) The ground bass piece gets more and more complex as it goes on. It can be developed by adding extra, decorative notes to the melody, using more advanced harmonies and adding more instruments to give a richer texture.

A Cadenza is where a Soloist can Show Off

1) A cadenza is a bit of music that's played by a soloist, usually in the middle of a concerto (see Section 5 of the Core Book).

2) Almost all concertos have a cadenza — it allows the soloist to show off their technique.

3) Cadenzas started out as improvisations on the main themes of a piece, but now most of them are written out by the composer. However, different musicians will interpret the cadenza in their own way.

Freshly ground bass — it goes all powdery...

Have a listen to a couple of different musicians' performances of Haydn's Trumpet Concerto in E flat major — the cadenzas will sound different in each one, even though the soloists are playing the same notes.

Popular Song Forms

It's not just Classical music that follows set structures — pop songs do as well.

Pop Songs usually have an Intro

Pop tunes almost always start with an intro. It does two jobs:

- It often uses the best bit from the rest of the song to set the mood.
- It grabs people's attention and makes them sit up and listen.

Most Pop Songs have a Verse-Chorus Structure

After the intro, the structure of most pop songs goes verse-chorus-verse-chorus.

- All the verses usually have the same tune, but the lyrics change for each verse.
- The chorus has a different tune from the verses, usually quite a catchy one. The lyrics and tune of the chorus don't change.
- In a lot of songs the verse and chorus are both 8 or 16 bars long.

'I Can't Get No Satisfaction' by the Rolling Stones has a verse-chorus structure.

The old verse-chorus thing can get repetitive. To avoid this most songs have a middle 8, or bridge, that sounds different. It's an 8-bar section in the middle of the song with new chords, new lyrics and a whole new feel.

The song ends with a coda or outro that's different to the verse and the chorus. You can use the coda for a big finish or to fade out gradually.

Pop Songs can have Other Structures too

For example:

CALL AND RESPONSE

This has two bits to it. Part 1 is the call — it asks a musical question. Part 2, the response, responds with an answer (p.29).

RIFF

A riff is a short section of music that's repeated over and over again (a bit like an ostinato — see p.33). Riffs can be used to build up a whole song. Each part, e.g. the drums or bass guitar, has its own riff. All the riffs fit together to make one section of the music. They often change for the chorus.

'Take a Bow' by Rihanna is an R&B ballad.

BALLADS

These are songs that tell stories. Each verse usually has the same rhythm and same tune.

32-BAR SONG FORM

This breaks down into four 8-bar sections. Sections 1, 2 and 4 use the main theme. Section 3 uses a contrasting theme, making an AABA structure. The 32 bars are repeated like a chorus. The verse is only played once — it's usually slowish and acts more like an introduction.

Verse — chorus — verse — chorus — tea break — chorus...

It's not just pop songs that follow these structures — songs from musicals do too. Have a listen to 'Defying Gravity' from the musical 'Wicked', 'I'm Reviewing the Situation' from 'Oliver!' and 'Any Dream Will Do' from 'Joseph and the Amazing Technicolour Dreamcoat' and try and spot some of these structures.

Revision Summary — Sections 5 & 6

Wow, look at that, you've reached the end of the book. Congratulations! But before you can celebrate and put on your dancing shoes (or curl up in your slippers), there's just time for one last Revision Summary. This one covers Sections 5 & 6, so you might need to look all the way back to Section 5 if you get stuck on the first few questions. Ooo, and because I was feeling particularly nice today, I've put together a little glossary for you at the back of the book to help you learn those tricky words.

1) Name four different African drums.
2) What is a balaphon?
3) In which country are sitars commonly played?
4) What effect do the 'sympathetic' strings on a sitar have?
5) How many strings does a tambura have?
6) What is a dayan?
7) Name three different types of Caribbean music.
8) Describe the four different sections of a modern salsa band.
9) What is timbre?
10) Explain how the sound is produced on:
    a) a string instrument,   b) a piano,   c) a brass instrument.
11) Give one way in which you could change the timbre of each of these instruments:
    a) a clarinet,   b) a trumpet,   c) a drum.
12) Name four different guitar effects.
13) Describe one difference between real and synthesized sounds.
14) What is sampling?
15) Describe how dynamics were used in:
    a) the Baroque period,   b) the Classical period,   c) the Romantic period.
16) How many sections are there in binary form?
17) How many sections are there in ternary form?
18) Describe the structure of rondo form.
19) What is call and response?
20) Explain what is meant by an arch-shaped melody.
21) What is theme and variation form?
22) Give four different ways you can vary a tune.
23) Name and describe the three different sections in sonata form.
24) Describe minuet and trio form.
25) What is a scherzo?
26) What's the difference between strophic and through-composed form?
27) What's a da capo aria?
28) Describe cyclic form.
29) What is basso continuo?
30) Explain how figured bass works.
31) Describe the structure of a ground bass piece.
32) What's a cadenza?
33) Describe verse-chorus structure.
34) Name three other structures often used in pop songs.

Air Guitar

Air guitar is a relatively new musical style. It developed about 25 or so years ago, when Mr. Osbourne was more famous than his wife and spent his time biting the heads off bats.

Air Guitar uses the Same Techniques as Real Guitar

First things first. Playing air guitar is exactly the same as playing a real guitar. The only difference is there's no guitar. So, like any beginner (real) guitarist, you need to learn some basic techniques:

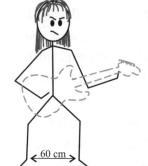

1) Learn how to hold your 'guitar'. Find one that matches your size, and practise holding it in the right position. Always practise this in front of a mirror.

2) Get the stance right. Your feet should be at least 60 cm apart*. For general posture ideas, think caveman/woman.

   * *This is only true if you're playing rock music from the 70s onwards. For example, if you were playing 50s-style rock'n'roll you would need an entirely different stance — feet together, no movement from waist down, top half of body swaying from left to right, cheesy grin...*

3) Make sure you always look like you're concentrating *really really* hard. This is particularly important during widdly bits.

4) Hair time. If you don't have long hair, it's very important that you pretend you do have long hair. Move the head forwards and backwards in time with the music, throwing your hair everywhere. If you're doing it properly you should soon notice your hair starting to stick to your sweaty face and get caught in your mouth and nose. Perfect this hair technique and you're well on your way.

You need to Learn the Three Classic Moves

The 'Down-on-One-Knee' Manoeuvre is Easy

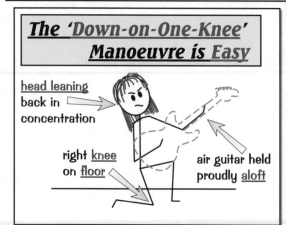

head leaning back in concentration

right knee on floor

air guitar held proudly aloft

'The Windmill' Takes a Bit More Practice...

right hand forming perfect circles

The trick is getting the circle to pass through the point where you would hit the strings (if you were playing a real guitar). This requires both technique and confidence. It's easy to look like an idiot if you mess it up.

...and you need Spandex Pants to do the 'Star Jump'

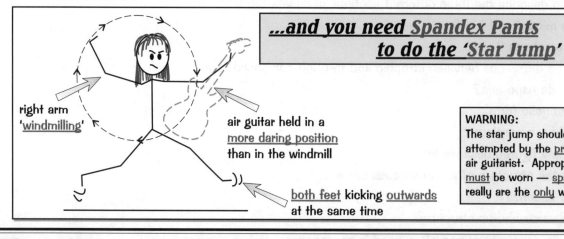

right arm 'windmilling'

air guitar held in a more daring position than in the windmill

both feet kicking outwards at the same time

WARNING:
The star jump should only be attempted by the professional air guitarist. Appropriate clothing must be worn — spandex pants really are the only way to go.

Air guitar — don't knock it till you've tried it...

And finally... I'd like to finish off the page with a list of recommended tunes to practise air guitar to.
1. Sweet Child O' Mine (G'n'R)   2. Eye of the Tiger (Survivor)   3. Bohemian Rhapsody (Queen)
4. Run to the Hills (Iron Maiden)   5. Livin' on a Prayer (Bon Jovi)   6. Money for Nothing (Dire Straits)

Glossary and Index

As I'm sure you're all-too-painfully aware, there's a staggering number of technical terms that you're expected to learn for GCSE Music. So I thought a bit of a glossary-type-thing wouldn't go amiss here...

Glossary and Index

D

da capo aria An **aria** in **ternary form**. 32
development The second section in **sonata form** where ideas are developed. 31
diatonic harmony When the notes in the accompaniment belong to the key of the piece. 13
diminuendo Get quieter. 27
diminution Dividing the length of notes in a tune to get a new version of it. The opposite of **augmentation**. 11
discords **Chords** that clash. 13
disjunct When there are big jumps between the notes in a melody. The opposite of **conjunct**. 18
dissonance **Chords** and **intervals** that clash. 13
distortion A guitar effect that distorts the note. 26
djembe Single-headed African drum played with the hands. 23
dominant The fifth note of a scale. 14, 28, 31
dominant key The key based on the fifth note of a scale. 14, 28, 31
donno An African drum shaped like an hourglass. Players hit it with a thin curved stick. 23
dotted rhythms When a dot is added to a note, it increases its length by half its value. 11
double stopping On a string instrument — when two strings are pressed at the same time so two notes can be played at once. 25
drone A long, held-on note, usually in the bass. 13, 21
drum fills Short drum solos in between sections of a piece, usually found in **pop** music. 12
dundun Double-headed African drum played with sticks. The types are doundoun, kenkeni and sangban. 23
duple metre Music with two equal beats in a bar. 10
dynamics How loud or quiet the music is. 21, 25, 27

E

electronic effects Effects used to change the **timbre** of instruments. 26
episode The contrasting sections in **rondo form**. 28
exposition The first section of **sonata form** where ideas are introduced. 31

F

falsetto When male singers sing notes in the female vocal range — much higher than their normal range. 25
families of instruments Groups of similar instruments, e.g. woodwind, strings, brass. 25
figured bass A type of notation often used for **continuo** parts. The bass notes are written on the stave, then numbers written underneath the notes tell the performers which chords to play. 33
film music 32
flanger A guitar effect that sounds a bit like a **phaser** but more intense. 26
free metre Music with no pattern to the beats. 10

G

glissando A slide between notes. 20
ground bass A repeating bass part that variations are played over the top of. 33
group performance (Unit 3) 7
guiro A **Caribbean instrument** that you scrape. 24

H

harmonium A keyboard instrument powered with air pumped by hand bellows. Used in Indian music. 24
harpsichord A keyboard instrument shaped like a **piano**. It was popular in the **Baroque** period. 27, 33
hemiola Where two bars of simple triple time are played as if they are 3 bars of simple duple time. 11
homophony Music where the tune is accompanied by **chords**, or where all the parts are playing the same rhythm. 16-17

I

imitation When a phrase is repeated with a little variation. It could be one instrument or voice imitating itself, or two or more imitating each other. 16
imperfect cadence A cadence that usually moves from chord I, II or IV to chord V. 29
improvisation Music that's made up on the spot by a performer, often based on a given chord progression or set of notes. 21, 33
Indian instruments 24
individual performance (Unit 3) 6
interval The gap between two notes, played one after another or at the same time. 13, 18
introduction Opening section of a song or piece. 31, 34
irregular metre Type of **metre** where the notes in a bar are grouped together to form uneven beats. 10

J

jazz Music with lots of **improvisation** and **syncopation**. 21

K

kagan A small, barrel-shaped African drum. 23
kidi A medium-sized, barrel-shaped African drum. 23
kora West African harp-like instrument. 23

L

layering Playing lots of **loops** at the same time. 16
listening to and appraising music (Unit 1) 2
loop A recording of a short section of sound that's repeated over and over again. 16, 26

Glossary and Index

M

major A key that sounds happy and bright. Uses notes from the major scale. **13-14**

maracas A **Caribbean instrument** that you shake. **24**

marcato Play every note with an **accent**. **20**

mbira African thumb piano. **23**

metre Pattern made by the beats in a bar. Can be **regular**, **irregular** or **free**. **10**

metronome marking A marking at the start of a piece that tells you how fast to play it. **10**

middle 8 An 8-bar **bridge** section in a **pop** song. Stops it from getting boring. **34**

minor A key that sounds sad and mournful. Uses notes from the minor scale. **13-14**

minuet and trio A piece in **ternary form**. Often used as the third movement of a **sonata** or **symphony**. **31**

modulation Changing key. **13-14, 28**

monophony Thin musical **texture** with just a tune and nothing else. **16**

musicals 34

mute Wooden, rubber or metal gadget used to dampen the sound of **brass** and **string** instruments. **25**

O

octave The distance from one note to the next note, up or down, with the same letter name (e.g. C to C). **13, 17, 26**

opera Drama set to music. **32**

ornaments Twiddly notes added to a tune to make it more interesting. **21, 30-31**

ostinato A repeated bass part. **33**

outro Another name for a **coda**. Used in **pop music**. **34**

P

pedal note A repeated note in the bass part. **13**

percussion instruments Instruments that make a sound when you hit or shake them **25**

perfect cadence A cadence going from chord V to chord I. **14**

perfect intervals The intervals between the first note of a scale and the fourth note, the first note and the fifth note and the **octave**. **13**

performance (Unit 3) 6-7

performing conventions (Unit 2) 5

phaser A guitar effect that creates a 'whooshing' sound. **26**

phrases A few bars or notes that are grouped together. A musical sentence. **20**

pitch shifting A guitar effect that adds harmonic interest. **26**

pivot chord A chord you use to modulate between keys. The pivot chord is the same in both keys. **14**

pizzicato 'Plucked'. A way of playing a **string instrument**. **25**

polyphony Musical texture where two or more different tunes are being played at the same time. **16-17**

polyrhythms When two or more different rhythms that fit together are played at the same time. **12**

pop Popular music. **29, 32, 34**

portamento A slide between notes. **20**

pulse The speed and pattern of the beats. **10**

Q

quadruple metre Music with four equal beats in a bar. **10**

R

raga A set of notes used in Indian music. **21**

realization An **improvisation** based on the **chords** given in **figured bass**. **33**

recapitulation The third section of **sonata form** where the ideas are played again. **31**

refrain The main theme in **rondo form**. **28**

reggae A type of Caribbean music. **24**

regular metre A type of **metre** where all the beats are the same length. **10**

reverb A guitar effect that adds an echo to the sound. **26**

rhythm'n'blues (R'n'B) A style of music from the 1950s and 60s that developed from **blues**. **19**

riff Repeated **phrase** played over and over again. Used in **jazz**, **pop** and rock music. **34**

Romantic Musical style from the mid-19th to early 20th century. It's very dramatic and expressive. **27**

rondo form A way of structuring music so you start with one tune, go on to a new one, go back to the first one, on to another new one, back to the first one, on to a new one... as many times as you like. **28**

round Another name for a **canon**. **16**

rubato You can be flexible with the speed of the music. **10**

S

sacred music Church music or religious music. **5**

salsa A type of music that comes from a mix of Cuban **son** and New York **jazz**. **24**

sample Short sections of recorded sound. **26**

sarangi A small, bowed string instrument with no frets. Used in Indian music. **24**

sarod An instrument like a small **sitar** with a fretless fingerboard. Used in Indian music. **24**

scalic A melody that moves using the notes of a scale. **18**

scherzo and trio Lively third movement of a **symphony** or **sonata**. **31**

Glossary and Index